Terrance Talks Travel:

The Quirky Tourist Guide to Wilmington & and the Cape Fear Coast, North Carolina

Terrance Zepke

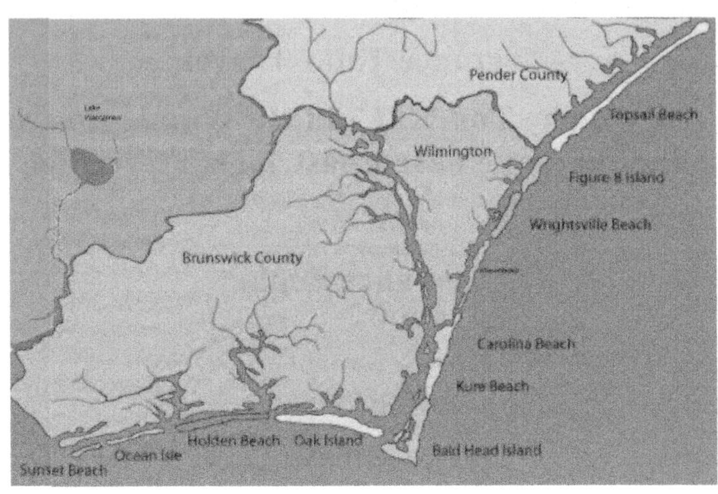
Pender County
Topsail Beach
Wilmington
Figure 8 Island
Wrightsville Beach
Brunswick County
Carolina Beach
Kure Beach
Holden Beach
Oak Island
Bald Head Island
Ocean Isle
Sunset Beach

All queries should be directed to: www.safaripublishing.net.

For more about the author: www.terrancezepke.com and www.terrancetalkstravel.com

Library of Congress Cataloging-in-Publication Data

Zepke, Terrance

Terrance Talks Travel: The Quirky Tourist Guide to Wilmington & the Cape Fear Coast, North Carolina

Travel-North Carolina. 2. Travel Guide-NC Coast. 3. Wilmington-NC. 4. Cape Fear Beaches. 5. Wilmington History & Folklore. 8. Cape Fear Coast Guidebook. 9. Wrightsville Beach. 10. Carolina Beach. 11. Kure Beach. 12. Fort Fisher. 13. Filmmaking. 14. Cape Fear River. I. Title.

ISBN: 9781942738787

Safari Publishing

First Edition

10 9 8 7 6 5 4 3 2 1

CONTENTS

Cape Fear River & Cape Fear Memorial Bridge, Wilmington

INTRODUCTION

My family had a home in the Wilmington area for many years. We loved it here! What makes it so great is the mild year-round climate (215 sunny days annually with an average of 64°F), a 230-block Historic District including its Downtown Riverwalk (rated #1 in the USA), fantastic dining options, the scenic Cape Fear River, nightlife, area beaches, lots of attractions, fun tours, and much more!

Plus, there is always something going on in the greater Wilmington area, such as the Azalea Festival, Wilmington Riverfest, and Enchanted Airlie; GEM Studios television and movie productions, beach celebrations, special events aboard the *USS Battleship NC* (permanently moored on the Cape Fear River), summer jazz series at Bellamy Mansion, Summer Tiki Shows, Sounds of Summer Concert Series, Free Fort Fisher Summer Concerts, Oceanic Summer Music Series, Port City Music Festival, Boogie in the Park Concert Series, hundreds of year round shows and plays at historic Thalian Hall, and special events and programs at the University of North Carolina Wilmington.

Wilmington is known as the "Hollywood of the East" and "Wilmywood" because it is the largest studio in America outside of Hollywood. There is always at least one movie or television show being filmed here—more than 400 so far! The biggest production filmed here to date was Marvel's Iron Man 3. That movie required the use of all ten studio soundstages. Don't be surprised if you spot a famous actress or director around town. Some have even moved here or bought vacation homes after falling under Wilmington's spell.

You can take a famous locations tour to see where some of these productions have filmed in the greater Wilmington area. Or you can take one of the many other tours offered, such as a spooky fun ghost walk, sunset sightseeing harbor cruise, *USS Battleship NC* tour, or a Bike & Brew Tour. Gem Studios offers tours of its production facility sometimes so you may get lucky and see a show or movie in progress.

Wilmington has a great music scene with live concerts being performed at various area locations most weekends, as well as many week nights during summer. Many renowned musicians have played in venues across greater Wilmington, such as the Avett Brothers, Five for Fighting, Lee Rocker of the Stray Cats, Josh Groban, Charlie Daniels, Trace Atkins, and Widespread Panic. There's even a School of

Rock Wilmington if you'd like to learn how to hone your skills to become a future rocker—all ages welcome!

There are so many great cafes, bistros, diners, restaurants, seafood shacks, bars, nightclubs, lounges, breweries, and coffee bars. No matter what kind of food is your favorite, this port city has it. A regret you will surely have as you pack to go home is that you were not able to try all the places on your list. But that just gives you a good reason to come back soon!

There are several significant beaches within a few miles of Wilmington. Also, there are dozens of parks, preserves, and refuges in the area. As if all of this is not enough, there are many good daytrip options, including Bald Head Island, New Bern, Beaufort, and Southport. North Myrtle Beach is only 59 miles south of Wilmington.

Best of all, there are lots of free things you can do in Wilmington that are so much fun you won't believe they're free, such as the 67-acre Airlie Gardens featuring twelve exotic gardens, a one-of-a-kind butterfly house, and free concert series; The Cotton Exchange, The Riverwalk, New Hanover County Arboretum, Masonboro Island Reserve, Fort Fisher Historic Site, Fort Fisher Recreation Area, and more!

Wilmington is a good place for all ages and interests, including small children, hard-to-please teenagers, and older adults. It is also suitable for all types of budgets with so many dining and lodging options. Plus, there are discounts and specials offered for many area attractions and tours, so be sure to ask.

Just be sure to make reservations and buy tickets in advance, especially during holidays and summer months. Now read on to discover how to make the most of your visit to the great Cape Fear Coast.

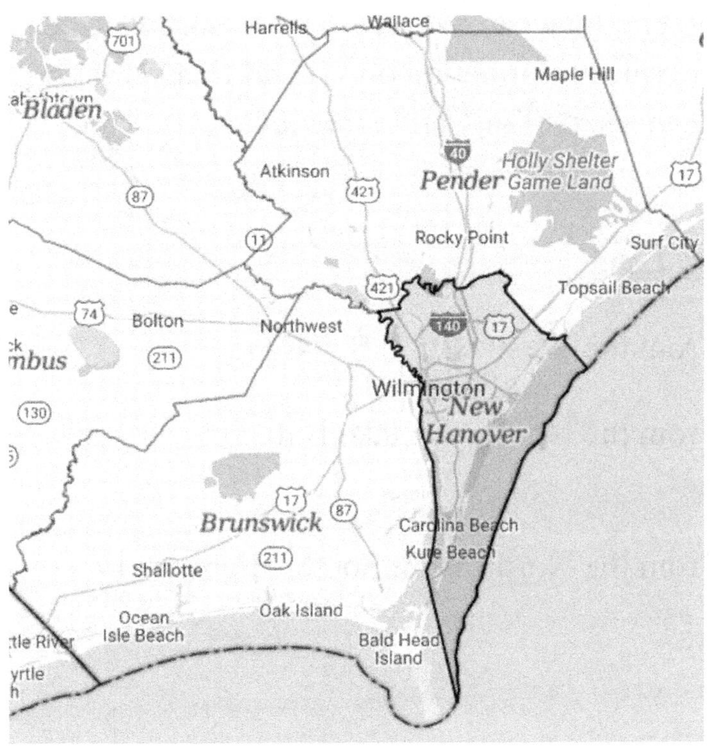

GETTING THERE

By Air

There is an airport, **Wilmington International Airport** (five miles north of downtown Wilmington), 1740 Airport Blvd, Wilmington.

There are direct flights to Wilmington from several major U.S. cities. The airport website provides information on ground transportation services, parking, and directions. www.flyilm.com

By Land

From the West: take U.S. 74/76

From the Northwest, take I-40, U.S. 117 & U.S. 421

From the Northeast & South, Highway 17

FYI: Wilmington is home to the second largest television and movie studio in the United States (California is #1).

Distance from Wilmington to...

Raleigh, NC=123 miles
Charleston, SC=167 miles
Charlotte, NC=203 miles
Atlanta, GA=413 miles
Jacksonville, FL=431 miles
New York City, NY=599 miles
Pittsburgh, PA=617 miles
Columbus, OH=663 miles
Miami, FL=780 miles

More Options

Amtrak offers direct service to Wilmington. https://www.amtrak.com/home.html

Greyhound Lines run buses to Wilmington. There is a station at 505 Cando St, Wilmington. https://www.greyhound.com/en-us/bus-station-340901

By Private Boat

Experienced boaters can reach this port city by private boat. Self-service day docking only is available at no cost at the **Wilmington City Docks**, 54 N. Front Street, https://www.wilmingtonnc.gov/departments/parks-recreation/docking

Wrightsville Beach Marinas:

Atlantic Marine, 101 Keel Street, https://atlanticmarine.com/

Bridge Tender Marina, 1418 Airlie Road, http://www.bridgetendermarina.com/

Dockside Marina, 1306 Airlie Road, http://www.thedockside.com/marina/

Seapath Yacht Club/Transient Dock, 330 Causeway Drive, https://seapathyachtclub.com/

Wrightsville Beach Marina & Transient Dock, 1 Marina Street, https://www.wrightsvillebeachmarina.com/

Also, there are marinas at Carolina and Kure Beaches, https://www.wilmingtonandbeaches.com/about/getting-around/marinas/

By Ferry Service

The NC DOT Ferry Division runs a public ferry service from Southport-Fort Fisher. When the ferry docks, you can drive from Fort Fisher to Wilmington. It is seventeen miles north via Carolina Beach. https://www.ncdot.gov/travel-maps/ferry-tickets-services/routes/

Getting Around Wilmington

Wave Transit is the city public transit service that includes buses, shuttles, and trolleys. www.wavetransit.com

FYI: If you have an electric or hybrid vehicle, there is a charging station at the Market Street Parking Deck (downtown).

Rideshare: Uber and **Lyft** are available in Wilmington.

There are taxis and car services:

Airport Taxi Service, https://www.ilmtaxiservice.com/

Angel's Taxi, www.angelstaxi.com

RSVP Black Car Service, https://rsvpblackcar.com/

The Transporter, www.nctransporter.com

FYI: The Waze travel app provides real time traffic updates and notifies users of area accidents and roadwork, as well as ETA. https://www.waze.com

Water Taxi: Bizzy Bee,
https://www.wilmingtonwatertaxi.com/
Bizzy Bee has three downtown landings: The Battleship NC, Market Street and Chandlers Wharf on the Riverwalk between Orange and Ann St. Private taxi service can be arranged, as well.

Parking. Most street parking is metered, but is free on holidays, weekends, and after 6:30 p.m. weekdays. There are several public parking lots and garages in Wilmington. The parking decks on 2nd Street are free for the first ninety minutes. https://www.wilmingtonnc.gov/departments/city-manager/parking

Visitor Welcome Centers

Wilmington and Beaches Convention and Visitors Bureau provides tourist information weekdays until 5 p.m. 1 Estell Lee Pl Unit 201, Wilmington, NC 28401. https://www.wilmingtonandbeaches.com/

The riverfront **Wilmington Visitor Information Booth** is located along the Riverwalk at the foot of Market Street and Water Street. Check their website for seasonal hours of operation. https://www.wilmingtonandbeaches.com/about/area-information/vic/

Wrightsville Beach Chamber & Visitor Center located at 305 W. Salisbury Street in Wrightsville Beach's Historic Square. https://wrightsville-beach.wilmingtonandbeaches.com/about/island-info/visitor-information-center/

New Hanover County Towns & Communities:

Wilmington

Figure Eight Island

Wrightsville Beach

Carolina Beach

Kure Beach

Fort Fisher

Masonboro Island (uninhabited)

FYI: Located on the Southeastern tip of North Carolina, historic New Hanover County is bordered by 31 miles of Atlantic shoreline on one side and the tranquil waters of the Cape Fear River on the other. Nearby towns, such as Southport, Ocean Isle, Bald Head Island, (Brunswick Co.) Topsail Beach, and Surf City (Pender Co.) are not in New Hanover County.

However, all three counties (New Hanover, Brunswick, and Pender) comprise the Cape Fear area.

Wilmington Area Beaches

Wrightsville Beach is the closest to Wilmington (eight miles away) and also the most upscale of the area beaches. Best things to do or see at this three-mile-long beach: Johnnie Mercers Fishing Pier, Wrightsville Beach Museum of History, Wrightsville Beach Park, Crystal Pier, and Stanback Coastal Education Center. Shell Island Resort, at the north end of Wrightsville Beach, is the biggest and oldest resort at this beach.

Carolina Beach (twelve miles from Wilmington) is a laid back, sort of "retro" beach town. Best things to do or see at this 2.5-mile-long beach: Carolina Beach State Park, Carolina Beach Boardwalk, Carolina Beach Fishing Pier, Carolina Beach Lake, Carolina Beach Arcade, Freeman Park, Federal Point Historic Preservation Society Museum, and Island Greenway.

Kure Beach is the smallest and quietest of the area beaches. Like Carolina Beach, it feels like a throwback to the "good old beach days." Best things to do or see at this 565-acre beach: Kure Beach Pier (one of the oldest piers on the Atlantic Coast), Ocean Front Park, Joe Eakes Park, and Hi-Tech Arcade.

Masonboro Island is an uninhabited, 8.5-mile barrier island (the largest barrier island in the area) that is accessible only by boat. There are public and private boat ramps in Wrightsville Beach and Carolina Beach. You can also canoe, kayak, swim, and camp out on the island, which feels like your own private oasis! There is a beach with good shelling and there is wildlife, especially birds, sea turtles, and an occasional alligator. Just be aware of tide times when coming and going from the island.

Figure Eight Island is a private, gated 1,300-acre island. It has five miles of pristine beaches, but the only way to gain access is to be invited by a property owner or to rent property here. Figure Eight Island real estate is among the highest priced in the state with prices starting at two million dollars. CEOs, politicians, and celebrities own homes here. There are no commercial businesses of any kind on Figure Eight Island, such as shopping centers, hotels, or restaurants.

Fort Fisher, at the end of Pleasure Island, extends two hundred acres. It is owned by the N.C. Division of Parks & Recreation. You can drive on the beach that is within the recreation area, as long as you have a permit and four-wheel drive. Things to see and do at this six-mile beach: Fort Fisher Recreation Area, Fort Fisher State Historic Site that includes a small part of the original fort, visitor's center, boardwalks for nature and wildlife viewing, boating ramp, paddling launch, and the North Carolina Aquarium at Fort Fisher featuring sharks, sea otters, sea horses, stingrays, eels, and sea turtles. You can catch the ferry over to Southport (35-minute ride) or walk over to Bald Head Island via a land bridge.

FYI: If you bring your dog to the beach, remember that he can get dehydrated, sunburn (especially light-colored dogs and pink skin that shows) and suffer a sunstroke just like humans. Also, the sand (and concrete and asphalt) is very hot for their paws

Cape Fear Beaches outside of New Hanover County:
Onslow and Pender Counties (north of Wilmington): Topsail Island (Surf City, Topsail Beach, and North Topsail).
Brunswick County (south of Wilmington): Oak Island (includes Caswell Beach), Holden Beach, Ocean Isle Beach, and Sunset Beach

Cape Fear Piers

Most of these are fishing piers and charge a fee to gain access.

Carolina Beach Fishing Pier

Crystal Pier (Wrightsville Beach)

Holden Beach Pier

Johnnie Mercers Pier (Wrightsville Beach)

Kure Beach Pier

Oak Island Pier

Ocean Crest Pier (Oak Island)

Ocean Isle Beach Pier

Sunset Beach Pier

Surf City Ocean Pier

Oak Island Lighthouse was the last one built in North Carolina (1958)

FYI: There are three Cape Fear lighthouses, including Bald Head "Old Baldy" Lighthouse, Oak Island Lighthouse, and Price's Creek Lighthouse. While Oak Island and Old Baldy are open to the public, Price's Creek is on private property and is not accessible. However, you can get a glimpse of it from the ferry.

Cape Fear Fishing

There are plenty of fishing options in the greater Wilmington area, but you must obtain a fishing license to legally do so unless you are fishing from a pier that charges a fishing fee or if you go on a fishing charter. Both of these have special commercial licenses that include these situations.

Check out this handy area fishing guide to find out about fishing charters, fishing licenses, area boat ramps, and more, www.capefear-nc.com/cape-fear-fishing-guide.html

Parks, Preserves, Refuges, & Recreational Areas

Airlie Gardens encompasses 67 acres of lush gardens and lakes. There are thousands of colorful azaleas and camellias. The ancient Airlie Oak Tree dates back to 1545. It is amazing! Airlie Gardens is also home to the only 2700-square-foot butterfly house in this area. Also, they have a native wildlife exhibit filled with terrariums and an aquarium. Enjoy this special place on foot using the walking trails or enjoy a scenic tram ride. Special seasonal events include bird

walks, summer concert series, and Enchanted Airlie, a spectacular holiday lights celebration. 300 Airlie Road, Wilmington, NC 28403. www.airliegardens.org

Bluethenthal Wildflower Preserve is a ten-acre wooded habitat at the University of North Carolina Wilmington. UNCW, 601 S College Road, Wilmington, NC 28403. https://uncw.edu/physicalplant/arboretum/bluethenthal.html

Cape Fear Museum Park has hands-on exhibits, gardens featuring native and adaptive plants, and educational activities. Located at the corner of 8th and Market Streets adjacent to Cape Fear Museum, the park is open from dawn to dusk and is free for everyone to enjoy. 814 Market Street, Wilmington, NC 28401. https://www.capefearmuseum.com/museum-park/

Carolina Beach Lake Park has four gazebos, restrooms, a sheltered picnic area, playground, an amphitheater and a walking path that circles the lake. Paddleboats are available to rent seasonally or enjoy a kayak outing. The park has many special events, such as a Farmers Market, Sunday Night Free Outdoor Movies, and "Light Up the Lake" Celebration in winter with thousands of twinkling lights all around the lake path. Atlantic Avenue and S Lake Park Blvd., Carolina Beach, NC 28428.
https://www.carolinabeach.org/government/depa

rtments/parks-recreation/parks-and-trails/lake-park

Carolina Beach State Park covers 761 acres, which includes a handicapped accessible visitor's center with exhibits, fishing deck, marina/fuel dock, nine trails, a bike path, campsites, and comfortable cabins. Rangers hold regularly scheduled educational hikes and programs. 1010 State Park Road, Carolina Beach, NC 28428.

www.ncparks.gov/carolina-beach-state-park/home

Empire Park is a 33-acre park with 18 tennis courts, a clubhouse, basketball courts, large dog park equipped with a shade canopy and benches, and a large playground suitable for children of all ages. The park also offers shelters with picnic tables, restrooms, and the Gary Shell Cross City Trail. 3405 Park Avenue, Wilmington, NC 28403.
https://www.wilmingtonnc.gov/departments/par

ks-recreation/tennis-pools/althea-gibson-tennis-complex

Fort Fisher State Historic Site has a handicapped accessible Visitor's Center, gift shop, and exhibits. There is a scenic trail that encircles the remains of the fort along the ocean side. 1610 Fort Fisher Blvd., Kure Beach, NC 28449.
https://historicsites.nc.gov/all-sites/fort-fisher

FYI: Fort Fisher is the location of the Civil War's biggest Amphibious Battle.

Fort Fisher State Recreation Area includes six miles of protected shoreline spanning from the Atlantic Ocean to the Cape Fear River with 288 acres of seashore, marsh trails, and observation deck. See where the Hermit of Fort Fisher once resided. Surf fishing is allowed with a fishing permit. Four-wheel drive vehicles are allowed with a permit. Leashed dogs are allowed. Parking, changing rooms, showers, restrooms, picnic areas with grills, a boat ramp, and paddling launch are also available. 1000

Loggerhead Road, Kure Beach, NC 28449. https://www.ncparks.gov/fort-fisher-state-recreation-area/home

Freeman Park is located at the north end of Carolina Beach and is usually not too busy even during the summer. It's a great place to swim, surf, kayak, go boating, crabbing or fishing. 1818 Canal Drive, Carolina Beach, NC 28428. www.carolinabeach.org/visitors/freeman-park

Gary Shell Cross-City Trail is a 15-mile primarily off-road, multi-use trail which provides bicycle and pedestrian access to recreational, cultural and educational destinations in Wilmington. When finished, the Gary Shell Cross-City Trail will provide a bicycle and pedestrian connection from Wade Park, Halyburton Park and Empie Park to the Heide-Trask Drawbridge at the Intracoastal Waterway. City-Wide, Wilmington, NC 28401. See their website for parking information and updates. https://www.wilmingtonnc.gov/departments/parks-recreation/gary-shell-cross-city-trail

Greenfield Park includes Greenfield Lake. The 250-acre park has tennis courts, skate park, outdoor amphitheater, boat rentals, picnic shelters, grills, restrooms, fishing dock, and a scenic five-mile biking/walking trail. 1739 Burnett Blvd., Wilmington, NC 28401. www.wilmingtonnc.gov/departments/parks-recreation/parks

Cypress trees in Greenfield Lake

Long Leaf Park offers paved trails which are perfect for biking, walking, or jogging. It also has soccer fields, softball fields, baseball fields, a basketball court, a volleyball court, tennis courts, picnic shelters, a pond, gazebo, off-leash dog park, and a large playground with a splashpad. 314 Pine Grove Drive, Wilmington, NC 28409. https://parks.nhcgov.com/parkinformation/locations/

Masonboro Island Reserve (8.4 miles long) is the longest, undisturbed barrier island along this stretch of coastline. Take a boat cruise or nature tour to explore and enjoy this special ecosystem. Masonboro Island can only be reached by boat, kayak, or canoe. There are public and private boat ramps at Wrightsville and Carolina Beaches. There are also private ferry services to the Reserve. Masonboro Island, Wilmington, NC 28409. https://deq.nc.gov/about/divisions/coastal-management/nc-coastal-reserve/reserve-sites/masonboro-island-reserve

New Hanover County Arboretum is seven acres full of different kinds of gardens, a Japanese tea house, children's cottage, gazebo, walking bridges, fountains, sculptures, scenic sitting areas, and a Koi pond. 6206 Oleander Drive, Wilmington, NC 28403. https://arboretum.nhcgov.com/

Ogden Park features a dog park, pond, picnic shelters, restrooms, a playground, walking trail and exercise station, tennis courts, baseball fields, a softball field, basketball court, soccer/football fields, youth football stadium, nature trail, and a state-of-the-art skate park. 615 Ogden Park Drive, Wilmington, NC 28411. https://parks.nhcgov.com/parkinformation/locations/

Piney Ridge Nature Preserve & Stanley Rehder Carnivorous Plant Garden is situated on 29 acres with a handicapped accessible walking trail, wooden observation decks, and a collection of native carnivorous plants such as pitcher plants and Venus flytraps. 3800 Canterbury Road, (behind Alderman Elementary School).
https://www.wilmingtonnc.gov/departments/parks-recreation/parks/piney-ridge-nature-preserve

The River to Sea Bikeway is an eleven-mile on and off-road bicycle route that follows the Historic Beach Trolley Line, which was used to transport vacationers from downtown Wilmington to Wrightsville Beach. This trail begins at the foot of Market Street at the Riverwalk.

Story Park at the Library features hands-on learning for all ages with four demonstration gardens, giant musical instruments, a StoryWalk®, and a life-sized chess and checker board. It is downtown at the corner of 3rd and Chestnut Streets. 201 Chestnut Street, Wilmington, NC 28401. https://libguides.nhcgov.com/storypark

Wrightsville Beach Loop is a scenic 3-mile loop that is suitable for walking, biking, and jogging). 1 Bob Sawyer Drive, Wrightsville Beach, NC 28480. https://www.townofwrightsvillebeach.com/181/Parks-Recreation

Wrightsville Beach Park has basketball courts, tennis courts, pickleball courts, volleyball pits, a softball field, an area for soccer or flag football, a recreation room, the Wrightsville Loop, and a playground designed for children with disabilities. Farmers Market, Summer Outdoor Concert Series, and Bark in the Park (Dog Agility) are just a few of the special events held here annually. 1 Bob Sawyer Drive, Wrightsville Beach, NC 28480. https://www.townofwrightsvillebeach.com/181/Parks-Recreation

Zeke's Island Reserve is 1,635 acres of barrier reef, tidal flats, salt marshes, dunes, and beaches. This is one of the most important shorebird feeding habitats on the East Coast. Bird species, such as black-bellied plovers, white ibis, black ducks, and great blue herons have been seen at Zeke's Island. Hwy 421, off of Kure Beach, NC 28449.
https://deq.nc.gov/about/divisions/coastal-management/nc-coastal-reserve/reserve-sites/zekes-island-reserve

Best Bird Watching

The **North Carolina Birding Trail** reveals the best places in the state to see birds and provides information about how to get there and what to look for. There are 20 sites in Brunswick, Pender, and New Hanover Counties with nine in Wilmington: Airlie Gardens, Greenfield Park, Oakdale Cemetery & Smith Creek Park), Carolina Beach (Carolina Beach State Park), Kure Beach (Fort Fisher State Historic Site & Fort Fisher State Recreation Area), and Wrightsville Beach (Mason Inlet Waterbird

Management Area & Masonboro Island Reserve). www.ncbirdingtrail.org

More Resources

The Cape Fear Audubon Society offers guided field trips throughout the year. Check their website for a calendar of events. www.capefearaudobon.org

Halyburton Park in Wilmington provides a variety of nature and birding programs, as well as field trips for children and adults, such as kayaking adventures and nature-themed arts and crafts projects for kids.

Wild Bird and Garden in Wilmington and Southport schedules local and out-of-town birdwatching trips throughout the year, including weekly walks in Airlie Gardens. www.wildbirdgardeninc.com

FYI: New Hanover County Parks & Gardens oversees twenty-five parks and athletic facilities. This includes 2,800 acres of green space, sporting areas, boat ramps, fishing areas, public spaces, walking trails and non-park properties, such as Airlie Gardens. Visit https://parks.nhcgov.com/park-information/locations/ **to find a list of all parks and recreation areas or visit** https://parks.nhcgov.com/wp-content/uploads/2022/01/2021-Parks-Brochure-Downsized.pdf **for a printable map with all park locations.**

Cape Fear Memorial Bridge

Fast Facts:

County: Wilmington is in New Hanover County and it is the county seat. Neighboring counties that are also part of the Cape Fear Coast include Brunswick and Pender.

Size: Wilmington encompasses 53 square miles and is home to the largest port in North Carolina.

Population: Wilmington has a population of 115,910 people (according to the 2020 U.S. Census), making it the eighth largest city in North Carolina.

Area: Wilmington is flanked by the Cape Fear River to the West and the Atlantic Ocean to the East. Wrightsville Beach is the closest beach, just eight miles east of Wilmington's Historic District.

Time Zone: Eastern Standard Time

Average Temperatures: Spring: 73°| Summer: 87°| Fall: 76°| Winter: 58°

The average ocean temperature for Wrightsville Beach is 68°.

Language: English

History: Wilmington was first populated by various Native American tribes. The first explorer to discover it was Giovanni da Verrazano in the late 16th century. The area was officially colonized in the 1720s, when an English settlement was established in the area, and by the 1730s, the area along the riverfront was named "New Town" By 1740, the area had taken a new name, Wilmington, in honor of the Earl of Wilmington in England, Spencer Compton. The proximity to the Cape Fear River helped the town grow into a bustling port community.

FYI: The Greater Wilmington area is called the Cape Fear Coast. The name, Cape Fear, comes from the 1585 expedition of Sir Richard Grenville. Sailing to the area, his ship became caught in the cape. Some of the crew were afraid they would sink at "Cape Fear."

In 1964, a four-legged tower resembling a Texas style oil-drilling platform was outfitted with a beacon and activated. The **Frying Pan Shoals Light Tower** is located at Frying Pan Shoals, which is roughly 39 miles southeast of Southport and 32 miles from Bald Head Island. It was decommissioned in 2003 and has been privately owned since 2009. https://fptower.org

Mitchell-Anderson House

Wilmington architecture: Classic Wilmington architecture is Georgian, Colonial Revival, and Neoclassical, which you will see lots of examples of in its 230-block historic district. The Mitchell-Anderson House (1738) is the oldest surviving structure in Wilmington. The home is a Georgian style house that was built for Edward Mitchell, a carpenter and planter from Charleston.

FYI: Check out these Wilmington area webcams,

www.surfchex.com/cams/wrightsville-beach/

TERRANCE'S TOP TEN PICKS

1. **Explore the Museum of the Bizarre**. The museum is small but so is the admission cost and it is a cool place to spend a hot afternoon. My favorite exhibits are the Fort Fisher Mermaid, Chupacabra Hand, Crystal Skull of Knowledge, and numerous movie props. There's are games, interactive exhibits, a mirror maze, and laser vault. 201 S. Water Street. https://www.museumbizarre.com/

2. **Spend some time exploring the Stanley Rehder Carnivorous Plant Garden**, the only one of its kind in this area. This is an unusual kind of garden featuring only carnivorous plants, such as pitcher plants, sundews, and Venus flytraps. It's a fun way to enjoy the great outdoors. It is meant to be explored on your own by reading the signs, meandering along the walking trails and enjoying the overlooks. The garden is open every day but if you

prefer a guided tour, free plant hikes are offered on Saturday mornings. This unique garden is part of the Piney Ridge Nature Reserve, which extends almost forty acres. One caveat: Do not pick any of the plants. It is a felony to remove any carnivorous plants in North Carolina. Oh, and one more thing, wear close-toed shoes. These are carnivorous plants, after all! FREE. 3800 Canterbury Road, (behind Alderman Elementary School). https://www.wilmingtonnc.gov/departments/parks-recreation/parks/piney-ridge-nature-preserve

This is one of the few places in the region where Venus Flytraps grow wild. They are protected by North Carolina law.

3. **Learn a new and unusual skill!** Attend the **N.C. Ukulele Academy** (203 Racine Drive, #205, www.aloahu.com).

   Or if you prefer you can take some classes at **Cape Fear Circus Arts.** The school specializes in trapeze and aerial skills classes, so I hope you're not afraid of heights or assuming awkward positions!

Classes take place at different locations in the Wilmington area.

https://www.capefearcircusartsstudio.com/

The School of Rock Wilmington is for those who were born to rock. See if you have what it takes,

www.schoolofrock.com

4. **Camp overnight at the remote Masonboro Island Reserve.** This is the largest and most pristine barrier island in the area. You can take a tour but the best way to enjoy Masonboro is to explore on your own. Bring a picnic if coming during the day or bring camp food for overnight stays. There is wildlife to see, such as sea turtles, American oystercatchers, and an occasional alligator. Also, you can go fishing, crabbing, shelling, sunbathe, swim, play games, tell camp stories, or organize an eco-scavenger hunt if you have kids. Located five miles SE of

Wilmington, Masonboro Island Reserve can only be reached by boat. There are public and private boat ramps in and near Wrightsville Beach and Carolina Beach and at the New Hanover County Trails End Park. There are also private fee ferry services to the reserve. Boats usually land on the beaches along the north and south sound side of the island. Trails allow visitors to walk across the island to access the beach. https://deq.nc.gov/about/divisions/coastal-management/nc-coastal-reserve/reserve-sites/masonboro-island-reserve

Or if you prefer a one-hour cruise tour to the island:
https://wrightsvillebeachscenictours.com/product/masonboro-cruise/

5. **Enroll in Sea Turtle Camp.** It is the best hands-on experience for kids of all ages, especially teens and pre-teens (sorry, no adults allowed!). Participants will work with the Sea Turtle Rescue and Rehabilitation Center to rescue and release live sea turtles. In addition to learning about local marine biology, you will also enjoy beach walks, surfing, and paddleboarding. There's also a Scuba Camp. www.seaturtlecamp.com

6. **Visit the only Japanese gaming parlor in North America.** Pachinko World offers retro pinball games from the 1940s – 2018. Pachinko grew in popularity in Japan following WWII and remains a very popular past time there. Arcade games cost just a quarter and pachinko just two cents per ball! 2591 S. 17th Street, Wilmington

www.facebook.com/PachinkoWorld
www.pachinkoworldusa.com

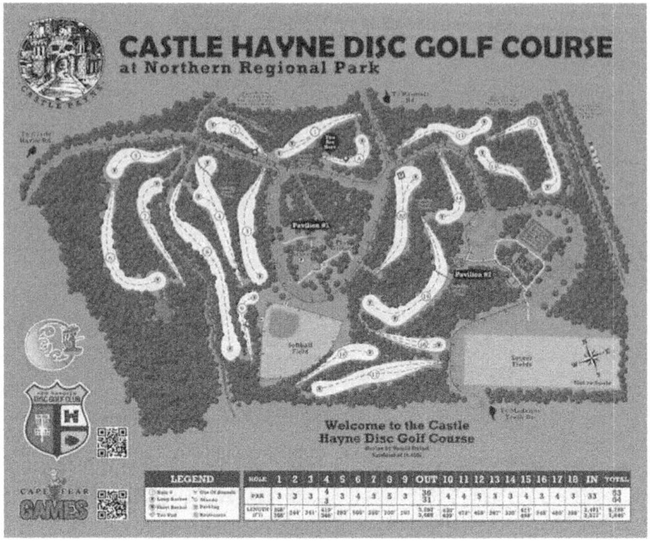

7. **Wilmington weather is perfect to enjoy one of the latest and greatest crazes in America**—disc golf. There are four disc golf courses in the area and all are free and fun! You will need your own disc(s), but you can buy them at Wilmington's Outdoor Provisions, Dick's Sporting Goods, and most area surf shops.

Here is a list of golf disc parks:

- **North Regional Park, Castle Hayne** (considered the best course in the area; see map on opposite page)
- **Joe Eakes Park, Kure Beach** (best for atmosphere with its coastal forest and sand fairways),
- **Arrowhead Park** (various elevations for extra challenge and picturesque park),
- **Good Hops Brewing, Carolina Beach** (you can legally pick up a craft beer inside and drink while you play or play while you drink—whichever you prefer!

8. **Meet movie stars or at least walk in their footsteps during a Hollywood Location Walk of Old Wilmington.** Many television shows and movies have been filmed here, such as Dawson's Creek, Matlock, One Tree Hill, Iron Man 3, The Conjuring, Halloween Kills, and the Scream series (earning it the nickname "Hollywood of the East" and "Wilmywood"). Tours depart from the riverfront at Market and Water Streets rain

or shine. Tickets can be purchased online or at Black Cat Gift Shop, 8 Market Street.

www.etix.com/ticket/v/4100/hollywood-location-walk-of-old-wilmington?cobrand=black

https://hauntedwilmington.com

One Tree Hill Bridge

Or take a free, self-guided tour (choose from five different themes, print out the location guide, and lace up your sneakers!)

https://www.wilmingtonandbeaches.com/things-to-do/tours-and-cruises/famous-film-and-tv-sites/

FYI: More than 400 film and television projects have been made at this 43-acre studio, which features ten sound stages totaling 250,000 square feet. It houses the largest special-effects water tank in North America. Screen Gem Studios tours are offered on occasion. I was given a tour of the studio and permitted on set when they were filming the final episodes of *Dawson's Creek*. I had lunch in the cast catering tent, but I wasn't allowed to ride from the set to the

lunch tent in the same car as Katie Holmes. Oh well, it was still a great day! Call before your visit to find out when tours are taking place and to reserve a spot: 910-343-3500. 1223 23rd Street North, Wilmington. https://euescreengems.com/wilmington-nc-studios/

9. **Enjoy a scenic harbor cruise.** Choose from a sunset cruise, wine tasting cruise, breakfast with the birds cruise, history cruise, or a nature cruise, www.wilmingtonwatertours.net.

Or if this is too mundane for you, try **BrewBoat Wilmington (Wilmington's only pedal pub on the water, www.brewboatnc.com) or Shamrock Sailing Adventures (www.shamrocksailing.com).**

10. **Find some ghosts!** Wilmington is one of the most haunted cities in America. During the Old Wilmington Ghost Walk you will learn about its many lingering spirits and most haunted places. Tours depart from the Ghost Walk sign on the

riverfront at Market and Water Streets. Tickets can be bought on line or at the walk if it is not sold out.

Private tours and Haunted Pub Crawls are also available. You may see many different kinds of "spirits" before the night is over! https://hauntedwilmington.com/ghost-walk.

Or peddle your way towards ghosts on an e-bike while on a **Wilmington History, Haunts & Breweries Tour**. More fun tour options are available at https://www.wilmingtonbikeandbrew.com

TOURISTY THINGS TO SEE & DO

Airlie Gardens is one of my favorite places in Wilmington. The 67-acre garden includes several seasonal gardens, historic buildings, a butterfly house, a native wildlife exhibit, a bug zoo, and a magnificent 500-year-old oak tree, Airlie Oak. They have a summer concert series, a monthly bird hike tour, weekly butterfly release show, Airlie Oyster Roast, and more family friendly events. 300 Airlie Road, Wilmington, NC 29804. www.airliegardens.org

Battleship NC is permanently moored at Eagle's Island, along the Cape Fear Riverfront. This historic battleship earned fifteen battle stars during its tenure (more than any other battleship during WWII). The *USS Battleship North Carolina* is a living history museum that is open to visitors. There is a large gift shop and special events are held seasonally. 1 Battleship Rd NE, Wilmington, NC 28401. www.battleshipnc.com

Bellamy Mansion (circa 1860) is an excellent example of pre-Civil War architecture. It housed Union troops when they briefly occupied Cape Fear. The home has been authentically restored and tours are offered of the house, as well as the carriage house, slave quarters, and exquisite gardens. 503 Market St, Wilmington, NC 28401. www.bellamymansion.org

Burgwin-Wright House Museum and Gardens is one of the oldest homes in Wilmington (1770) that is open to the public. This house museum includes lovely period antiques and furnishings. Self-guided or docent-led tours are available. During the American Revolutionary War, it served as headquarters for Lord Cornwallis. The house was built on top of the town's first jail. There were debtors' cells and cages for petty criminals near the space that is now the Burgwin-Wright House's art gallery. Executions were done at the jail's gallows before being moved just outside the city limits near Market Street and Fifth Avenue at a place commonly known as Gallows Hill. This means the house was built right on top of the site where many deaths had occurred. 224 Market St, Wilmington, NC 28401.
www.burgwinwrighthouse.com

Cameron Art Museum has many permanent and temporary exhibits showcasing the history of Cape Fear. A Civil War battle took place on the grounds where the museum now stands. Visitors can explore this fine arts museum at their leisure during a self-guided tour. 3201 S 17th St, Wilmington, NC 28412. www.cameronartmuseum.org

Cape Fear Museum dates back to 1898, making it one of the oldest museums in the area. Historic exhibits chronicle the rich history of Cape Fear. 814 Market Street, Wilmington, NC 29801. www.capefearmuseum.com

Children's Museum of Wilmington has fun educational and interactive exhibits (such as Animal Alley and Exploration Station), daily programs, special events, and field trips. 116 Orange St, Wilmington, NC 28401. www.playwilmington.org

The **Cotton Exchange** was built in the late 1800s to house the Cape Fear Flour and Pearl

Hominy Mill. Today, it is a shopping "mall" filled with boutiques, shops, salons, and dining venues. Be sure to check out the Wilmington Walk of Fame. 321 N Front St, Wilmington, NC 28401. www.shopcottonexchange.com

Downtown Riverwalk has been voted America's Best Riverfront by *USA Today* Reader's Choice Awards. This 1.7-mile boardwalk includes more than 200 shops, restaurants, attractions, and art installments. Many events are held on the Riverwalk throughout the year. This is the best view in the city and the city's #1 tourist attraction. https://www.wilmingtonnc.gov/visitors/riverwalk

Fort Fisher Historic Site is at the end of Kure Beach. Visitors can explore the remains of the Confederate fort along an interpretive trail. A visitors' center is also located on-site. This fort was one of the most important coastal strongholds for the Confederacy. 1610 Fort Fisher Blvd S, Kure Beach, NC 28449. https://historicsites.nc.gov/all-sites/fort-fisher

Battle of Fort Fisher

FYI: The Haw River and the Deep River flow together to form the Cape Fear River, which flows another 202 miles. It is the largest river system in the state with more than 6,500 miles of streams covering an area about the size of New Jersey. It provides water to many of the major cities in the state, including Greensboro, Durham, Chapel Hill, Fayetteville, and Wilmington. The southern portion of the estuary forms part of the Intracoastal Waterway. A series of locks and dams makes the river navigable from Wilmington to Fayetteville.

Hannah Block Historic USO Museum has WWII exhibits, a WWII gallery, and offers guided tours of this former USO club that is now a museum.
https://wilmingtoncommunityarts.org/museum/

Latimer House

Latimer House Museum and Gardens (1852) has fourteen rooms filled with 600+ antiques and historical objects! It is open to the public and well worth visiting. It also houses the Cape Fear

Historical Society. 126 S 3rd St, Wilmington, NC 28401. https://www.lcfhs.org/

Luna, a rare albino alligator

North Carolina Aquarium at Fort Fisher has lots of cool exhibits, such as the Cape Fear Shoals Habitat and Otters on the Edge. They also offer tours, adventures, daily programs, camps, special events (such as sleepovers and virtual programs). I recommend buying tickets online in advance of your visit if coming during peak times since this is a popular attraction. 900 Loggerhead Rd, Kure Beach, NC 28449. https://www.ncaquariums.com/fort-fisher

Oakdale Cemetery was part of the Rural Cemetery Movement that swept the U.S. in the mid-nineteenth century. These rural cemeteries took large tracts of vacant land and turned them into garden cemeteries. Ornamental plants and native vegetation grow around the plots making Oakdale one of the city's most beautiful spots.

War veterans from all branches of service, politicians, artists, architects, writers, merchants, planters, and victims of Yellow Fever epidemics, as well as a female Confederate spy, are buried here. 520 N. 15th Street, Wilmington, NC 28401. http://www.oakdalecemetery.org/

Orton Plantation has been a historic icon for many years. Thousands of tourists have visited and many scenes from television and movies have been filmed here, such as *Divine Secrets of the Ya-Ya Sisterhood, A Walk to Remember, One Tree Hill, Dawson's Creek, Hart of Dixie*, and

Matlock. Sadly, it was closed to the public in 2010 when the Laurence-Sprunt family sold the property to investment banker and conservationist, Louis Moore Bacon. He is a direct descendant of Roger Moore, the original builder of this home in 1725. Bacon and a team of experts are trying to grow Carolina Gold Rice, which hasn't been grown there since 1931. He has plans to restore the house and may re-open it to the public.

Poplar Grove Plantation was once an 835-acre plantation, is now a museum that shows what life was once like for area residents. Visitors can tour the main home and outbuildings. There is a farmer's market held here on certain days. Be sure to check their website for those dates and other special events and festivals, such as Goosebumps in the Grove! 10200 US-17, Wilmington, NC 28411. www.poplargrove.org

Thalian Hall for the Performing Arts was established in 1858 as an opera house for the Cape Fear area. It has been operational for more than 150 years. Thalian Hall hosts close to 500 events annually, ranging from concerts to comedy shows. 310 Chestnut St, Wilmington, NC 28401. www.thalianhall.org

Wilmington Downtown Historic District is one of the largest historic districts in the country—more than 230 city blocks! There are 875 contributing buildings, as well as 38 contributing sites, such as the Basilica Shrine of

St. Mary, New Hanover County Courthouse, and the Dudley Mansion. Just about any kind of tour you can think of is offered for the historic district, such as walking tours, ghost tours, Segway tours, bike tours, carriage tours, trolley tours, and even boat tours that launch from the Cape Fear Riverfront.

Wilmington National Cemetery was established after the Civil War. The five-acre cemetery is the permanent home to 557 soldiers who served during that war, as well as a total of 6,000 burial plots that include soldiers from virtually every American war and conflict. 2011 Market St, Wilmington, NC 28403. www.cem.va.gov/cems/nchp/wilmington.asp

FYI: There are many historic churches in Wilmington, including Grace United Methodist Church (1797), St. Mary Catholic Church, First Baptist Church (1808), First Presbyterian Church, and St. James Episcopal Church (1770) is the oldest in Wilmington, but the Temple of Israel (1876) is the oldest synagogue in the state and 10th oldest in continuous use in America.

Wilmington Railroad Museum is housed in one of the city's original brick warehouses. It has exhibits sharing the city's railroad history, which has the honor of being the longest single track railroad in the world at one time. There is a kid's hall, model train hall, old steam locomotive, ACL boxcar, and caboose that kids are allowed to board and explore. 505 Nutt St, Wilmington, NC 28401. https://www.wrrm.org

Wrightsville Beach Museum of History is located inside a historic (classic) beach cottage. There are artifacts, memorabilia, and exhibits

showcasing Wrightsville Beach history and heritage. Special events held seasonally, such as Ladies Night, Movie Night, and Kids Camp. 303 W Salisbury St, Wrightsville Beach, NC 28480. https://wbmuseumofhistory.com/

Special Activities & Tours

There are so many things to do along the Cape Fear Coast that you will have a good excuse to come back many times!

African American Heritage Walk is a self-guided walking tour that includes 37 African-American heritage sites. A pamphlet detailing the stops on this tour can be downloaded at https://www.wilmingtonnc.gov/home/showdocument?id=16 and virtual tours are available at http://www.aahfwilmington.org/aahmw_virtualexhibits.html

Blockade Runner Sailing School (Wrightsville Beach) is perfect for those yearning to learn to sail. Start with a one-hour fun sail to see if it's right for you. https://blockade-runner.com/sailing-school/

Cape Fear Riverboats has offered several options since 1987, including a Sightseeing Cruise, Sunset/Moonlight Cruise, and Black River Nature Cruise aboard the *Henrietta*. There is a bar on the boat where you can buy refreshments to enjoy during your outing. www.cfrboats.com

Daytrips from Wilmington: Southport, Beaufort and Shackleford Banks, Bald Head Island, New Bern, Emerald Isle, Cape Lookout

National Seashore, Croatan National Forest, and Moores Creek Battlefield.

Dead Crow Comedy Room if you need a good laugh. 511, N 3rd Street. Wilmington, NC 28401. www.deadcrowcomedy.com

DEFY Wilmington is an indoor thrill park with extreme dodgeball, battle beams, Ninja course, zipline, kids jump, and more. https://defy.com/defy-wilmington/

Downtown at Sundown are summer concerts held on Friday nights during the summer. They are free and fun for everyone! There are kid's

activities and food and beverage vendors. Local bands and talented musicians perform on the Downtown Riverwalk as the sun sets in the background. http://www.downtownatsundown.org/

Escape rooms are good for rainy days or for those who like to solve mysteries. Wilmington has several highly-rated escape rooms: Green Light Escape Room, The Exit Games, Port City Escape, Cape Fear Escape Rooms, and Xit Rooms.

Ghost Walk of Old Wilmington shares ghost stories while exploring downtown Wilmington. They also offer a Haunted Pub Crawl. https://hauntedwilmington.com/ghost-walk

Jungle Rapids Family Fun Park is a water park that also has bowling, laser tag, arcade games, rock climbing, and more. 5320 Oleander Drive, Wilmington, NC 28403. https://junglerapids.com/

Mahanaim Adventures Kayak Tour offers half-day or all-day kayak or canoe adventures for all ages. Gear, instruction, and food/drink are included. https://mahanaimadventures.com/

Noni Bacca Winery is a winery with a tasting room and extensive wine shop. The winery produces sixty different varieties of wine and earned 179 international medals of excellence, which are on display throughout the winery. 420 Eastwood Road, State 108, Wilmington, North Carolina 28403. www.nbwinery.com

Old Wilmington City Market opened in 1880 as a farmer's market. These days it features locally-owned specialty shops, arts and crafts galleries, and a coffee bar. Dogs are welcome! Near the Riverwalk. https://www.oldwilmingtoncitymarket.com/

Self-guided walking tour of historic Wilmington. If you prefer to explore on your own, download the Wilmington.tours app ($) onto your phone. The app offers several different tour options. The Old Wilmington tour includes sixteen locations with a short video sharing the history of each location. You can go as fast or as slow as you like to complete this tour.

Stand-up paddleboarding (SUP) is a fun water activity that almost anyone can do. There are several places in the Wilmington area where you can SUP, but one of the best is Wrightsville Beach. You can rent equipment and/or take lessons with Wilmington SUP, https://www.wrightsvillesup.com/

Tregembo Animal Park is a family-owned zoo established in 1952. It has 100 animal species, including a sloth, tiger, and snow macaques. 5811 Carolina Beach Rd., Wilmington, NC. http://www.tregemboanimalpark.com/

Wilmington's History, Haunts & Breweries E-Bike Tour includes stops at three Wilmington Craft Breweries and visits several significant historical sites. The half day ride is twelve miles but there are frequent stops and you are on an e-bike! https://www.wilmingtonbikeandbrew.com/

Wilmington Sharks are part of the Coastal Plain League. The baseball team plays all summer at Legion Stadium, a.k.a. "The Shark Tank." Thirsty Thursdays and Fireworks Fridays are especially popular nights. www.wilmingtonsharks.com

Wrightsville Beach Surf Camp offers kids, teens, and adult surf camps for beginners or advanced. Or you can just take a few lessons or rent equipment. https://www.wbsurfcamp.com/

Wrightsville Beach Mailbox is where you go to mail (or read) love letters. This tradition began in 2003 with one mailbox, one journal, one pen, and one encouraging sentence "Leave a note." Since that time, the mailbox has served as a busy repository for love notes, marriage proposals, and notes to lost loves. More than 200 journals have been filled out. There are two mailboxes nowadays due to an overwhelming lovelorn response. Letter writers pour out their hearts in the notes they leave here, hoping to mend a broken heart or maybe redirect Cupid their way.

Where to go? You will find the "love" mailboxes at the last beach access after Shell Island, which is on the north tip of Wrightsville Beach. It is a small stretch of undisturbed shoreline (from Shell Island Resort to Wrightsville Inlet) so at the very least you will enjoy a peaceful beach stroll. The original mailbox is now on display at the Wrightsville Museum of History.

FYI: Best place to watch the sunset is... anywhere along the Cape Fear Coast—duh! However, the south end of Wrightsville Beach is hard to beat. But it is a well-known fact so go early to guarantee you'll find parking. I also think that Sunset Cruises are pretty spectacular, as well as the view from the pier at Carolina Beach.

Wilmington has several local breweries. So if you like craft beer, take a brewery tour. Or take a trolley brew tour. Or take a brew cruise. Or take a brew and bike tour: **Haunted Pub Crawl, Port City Brew Bus, Sea Legs Pedal Pub, Wilmington Bike & Brew Tours, Roadies Local, Trolley Pub**

Wilmington, or **Wilmington Water Tours.** Or just stop in, have a seat, and enjoy a cold one: **Broomtail Craft Brewery, Wrightsville Beach Brewery, Edward Teach Brewing, Front Street Brewery** (oldest brewery in the area), **Flytrap Brewing** (specializes in American and Belgian-style ales), **Flying Machine Brewery, Good Hops Brewing, High Wire Brewing, Ironclad Brewery, Mad Mole Brewing** (only solar powered brewery in the area), **New Anthem Beer Project, Waterline Brewing, Wilmington Brewing Company**, and **Wrightsville Beach Brewery.**

FYI: The mobile phone app Untappd helps users track the beers they've already sampled or plan to sample at a later date. This app is a great way to stay connected with other beer lovers and track your "progress!"

Wilmington Scavenger Hunt is crazy fun. Twenty challenges. Two hours. One epic adventure. Your team will solve puzzles, complete challenges, and explore historic landmarks. www.scavengerhunt.com/locations/Wilmington_History_Scavenger_Hunt.html and **Wacky Wilmington Scavenger Hunt** provides a remote, but interactive, live host to assist and cheer you on as you participate in this two-hour adventure. https://www.wackywalks.com/Locations/Wilmington-NC

Wilmington Trolley Tour offers open-air trolley sightseeing tours around historic downtown Wilmington and also points out filming locations. https://wilmingtonnc.com/wilmington-trolley-company/

Wilmington Water Tours offers an Eagles Island Cruise, Down River Maritime History Cruise, wine tasting cruise, breakfast with the birds cruise, sunset cruise, and a Pirate School Cruise for kids. www.wilmingtonwatertours.net

Wrightsville Beach Bikes and Boards rents bikes, SUPs, surfboards, and kayaks by the hour, day, or by the week. https://www.wbbikesandboards.com/

Wrightsville Beach Jet Ski Rentals (www.wrightsvillebeachjetskirentals.com) or **Carolina Beach Jet Ski Rentals**, www.carolinabeachjetskirental.com

Billiards, Bowling & More

Battle House Laser Tag, 1817 Hall Drive, Wilmington.

Bluepost Billiards, 15 S. Water Street, Wilmington.

BreakTime Billiards Bar & Grill- Family Fun Center, 127 S College Rd, Wilmington.

Cardinal Lanes Shipyard, 3907 Shipyard Blvd #6152 and 7026 Market St, Wilmington.

Crossfire Indoor Paintball Park, 1413 Castle Hayne Drive, Wilmington.

Jelly Beans Family Skate Center, 5216 Oleander Drive, Wilmington.

RackM Darts & Billiards, 415 S. College Rd., Wilmington.

Retroscape Arcade, 1123 Princess Street, Wilmington.

BEST OF WILMINGTON

Tours, attractions, historic sites, and activities are addressed in the TOURISTY THINGS TO DO chapter. For more tourism information, visit www.wilmingtonandbeaches.com/about/area-information/vic/

BEST PLACES FOR SOUVENIRS: Blue Moon Gift Shops has more than 100 retailers specializing in handcrafted jewelry by local designers, local food specialties, artwork by local artists, home goods, and much more. www.bluemoongiftshops.com

RUNNER UP: Black Cat Shoppe is the place to go for those looking for unusual items, such as a Bigfoot Research Kit, Unicorn Discovery Kit, Dancing Hula Girl, funny novelties, nostalgia lunch boxes and toys, memorabilia from One Tree Hill (and other locally produced shows), and much more. www.theblackcatshoppe.com/

FYI: Major shopping complexes in Wilmington include Independence Mall, Cotton Exchange of Wilmington, Mayfaire Town Center, Hanover Center Shopping Mall, Long Leaf Mall, The Forum ILM, Chandler's Wharf, Landfall Shopping Center, Lumina Station, Front Street Center, University Centre, University Commons, and The Point at Barclay.

BEST PLACE TO STAY: More about lodging can be found in the ABOUT ACCOMMODATIONS chapter.

BEST LIVE MUSIC: The Shell is a relatively new live music venue right on the riverfront. They feature lots of artists, concerts, and a summer concert series. www.theshellwilmington.com

RUNNERS UP: Live at Ted's, Blind Elephant, Whiskey Tango Foxtrot, Duck and Dive Pub, Rusty Nail, Reggie's 42nd Street Tavern, and Jimmy's (Wrightsville Beach).

FYI: The Wilmington area has an awesome music scene. There are many good places to enjoy live music throughout the year.

BEST KARAOKE: Whiskey Tango Foxtrot offers karaoke every Thursday. www.whiskeytangofoxtrotnc.com

BEST BREW PUB: **Cape Fear Wine & Beer** features the best selection of beer and wine in Downtown Wilmington. Voted "Best Beer Selection" with craft beer, micro brews, wine tastings, and more. All the bartenders are Certified Cicerones so you're in good hands! Special events and/or special pricing are offered every day of the week. www.capefearwineandbeer.com

BEST TIKI BAR: **Low Tide Tiki Bar** (Carolina Beach), www.facebook.com/lowtidetikibar/
RUNNER UP: SeaWitch Café & Tiki Bar (Carolina Beach) www.seawitchtikibar.com

BEST PIER BAR: **High Tide Lounge** at the Carolina Beach pier

BEST DANCE SPOT: Ibiza Nightclub has DJ dance parties on Saturdays, karaoke on Wednesdays, drag shows on Friday and nightly drink specials and signature cocktails. www.facebook.com/ibizawilmington/

BEST BOOKSTORE: Pomegranate Books is a small indie bookstore that sells

popular fiction, nonfiction, kids and YA, and audiobooks. Zola Coffee & Teas is part of the bookstore, featuring iced herbal teas, hand-crafted spiced lattes, and more specialty drinks and pastries. https://pomegranatebooks.wordpress.com,
RUNNER UP: Old Books on Front Street specializes in rare and old books, www.oldbooksonfrontstreet.com

BEST SPA: Wilmington Massage & Wellness specializes in seven different kinds of massage therapy, infrared saunas, and skincare. www.rejuvilm.com/
RUNNER UP: Coastal Massage & Spa, www.Coastalmassagespa.com

BEST ROOFTOP BAR: Cloud 9 Rooftop Bar

BEST HAPPY HOUR: Dram and Morsel, www.dramandmorsel.com

BEST NIGHT CLUB: Prada boasts a professional light show, 30,000-watt sound

system, resident DJs, and bottle service.
http://wilmingtonnightclubs.com/pravda

BEST HIPSTER BAR: Blind Elephant,
www.blindelephantspeakeasy.com
RUNNER UP: KGB

BEST UNIQUE BAR: Juggling Gypsy is part café, part bar, part hookah lounge, part art gallery, and part music/performing arts venue. They host everything from art openings to beer tastings to live bands to masquerades. I don't know what else to say but that you just have to experience it for yourself.
www.jugglinggypsy.com

BEST SPORTS BAR: Hell's Kitchen,
www.hellskitchenbar.com
RUNNERS UP: Tilted Kilt Pub & Sports Bar and **Carolina Ale House**

BEST BEER GARDEN: Fermental was set inside a former 1950's service station in the Cargo District of downtown Wilmington but recently moved to a larger space. They offer an impressive assortment of draft beers and wines and host live music, food trucks, tastings, and special weekly events. Imported cheeses, cured meats, pickles, olives, and more nibbles are offered, as well as non-alcoholic beverages. www.fermental.com

BEST BEACH (Dive) BAR: Fat Pelican at Carolina Beach is always fun due to the eclectic crowd and the fact that it is at the beach. www.thefatpelican.com
RUNNER UP: The Last Resort (Carolina Beach)

BEST OVERALL BAR: The Blind Elephant is a speakeasy (prohibition bar) located in an abandoned alley in downtown Wilmington. It has a great ambience, specialty drinks, and is just a fun place to hang out. If you get a chance to go, ask

about their annual Great Gatsby Bash. www.blindelephantspeakeasy.com

BEST FARM TO TABLE (locally sourced): Circa 1922. They make everything from scratch and it is all sourced from the best local farmers and fishermen who deliver local seafood fresh off the boat. www.circa1922.com

BEST THAI: Indochine is an authentic Thai infusion restaurant that is so good that it is busy all the time, so be prepared to wait (but it is worth it). www.indochinewilmington.com

BEST CHEAP EATS: Hibachi Bistro serves cheap but yummy hibachi meals. www.hibachibistro.com

BEST SUSHI: Yosake serves the best sushi in town and a full pan-Asian menu with a special half price menu daily from 5-7pm. The bar serves an excellent selection of beer, wine, sake, and specialty cocktails. www.yosake.com

BEST RAW BAR: Shuckin' Shack Oyster Bar, www.shuckinshack.com

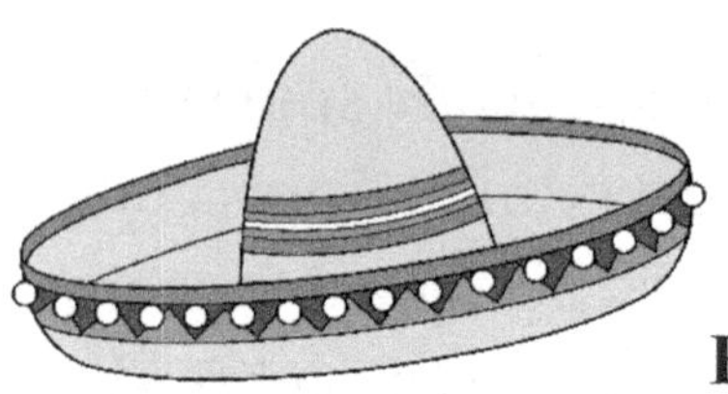

BEST MEXICAN: Taqueria Los Portales serves delicious authentic Mexican food (not American Mexican food), www.taquerialosportales.com

BEST SEAFOOD: Cape Fear Seafood Company looks a bit like a hole in the wall place but you can't beat its fresh seafood, extensive selection, or the price. It has been voted one of the best places for Shrimp & Grits in the Carolinas. Oh, and they have great drink specials daily, including a Hibiscus Margarita and Pineapple Citrus Sangria. www.capefearseafoodcompany.com

BEST PIZZA: Slice of Life (Wrightsville Beach) makes their own in-house dough and sauce and even has gluten-free and white pizza pies. www.grabslice.com

BEST COFFEE: Crush & Grind (Carolina Beach): serves gourmet coffee by day and becomes a chic wine bar by night—and they are eco-friendly.
RUNNERS UP: Cheeky Monkey Coffee, Three Friends Coffee, The Complex Bean, Luna Caffe, and **Bespoke Coffee & Dry Goods**

BEST DOUGHNUTS: **Britts Donuts** is an institution at Carolina Beach—opened in 1939. I'm not into doughnuts so I'm not a good judge, but everyone says they are the best and they certainly an icon here. And the doughnuts must be very good because glazed doughnuts is ALL they sell, besides coffee, soda, and milk. Be prepared to wait in line.
www.bittsdonutshop.com.
RUNNER UP: **Wake N' Bake Donuts**

BEST FONDUE: Little Dipper Fondue is a locally owned fondue restaurant with an intimate setting. They have specials every day of the week. If you're looking for something different (and yummy), look no farther! www.littledipperfondue.com

BEST ROMANTIC: Little Dipper Fondue is not your run of the mill fondue. They offer different selections and a special three-course dining experience that it is perfect for first dates or celebrating milestone anniversaries. www.littledipperfondue.com

BEST ITALIAN: Tarantelli's Ristorante Italiano is family-owned and has one of the most impressive menus I've ever seen (and I have seen many since Italian food is at the top of my favorite food list). Not only do they have excellent entrees, they have good starters, homemade desserts, and after dinner drinks. www.tarantellis.com

BEST LATIN AMERICA CUISINE: Ceviche's at Wrightsville Beach features authentic Latin American food, such as Jerk

Shrimp Skewers and Blackened Tuna, www.wbceviche.com

BEST BISTRO: Caprice Bistro is a Parisian-style bistro in historic downtown Wilmington that serves French food with an American twist. There is a dining room and a sofa bar lounge upstairs for a more intimate setting. Be sure and save room for dessert—they serve chocolate mousse! www.capricebistro.com

BEST DINER: Jimbo's has every kind of omelet you can imagine and standard diner menu, including chopped steak, pancakes, Belgian waffles, turkey club, salads, burgers, and platters. They have a good selection of sides and beverages, as well. www.jimbosbreakfastandlunch.com

BEST BRUNCH: Betsy's Crepes specializes in crepes and they are so good and they even have a DIY Bloody Mary Bar, www.betsyscrepes.com.

RUNNER UP: Blue Surf Café, www.bluesurfcafe.com

BEST FINE DINING: Elijah's is my favorite place. It is right on the waterfront with a fun, nautical theme (which makes sense since it is a seafood restaurant and the site of a former maritime museum). They serve the best chowder and their Cape Fear Stuffed Shrimp is awesome. www.elijahs.com

BEST APPETIZERS: Elijah's, www.elijahs.com

BEST ICE CREAM: Boombalatti's Homemade Ice Cream serves ice cream cones and pies, but their signature item is their banana split, www.boombalattis.com.

RUNNER UP: Kilwin's Ice Cream & Candy

BEST BAKERY: Apple Annie's Bake Shop specializes in pastries, cookies, and cheesecakes.

www.appleanniesbakeshop.com.
RUNNER UP: The Red Eye Bakery specializes in cinnamon rolls, biscuits, breads, and cookies.

BEST BURGER: The Original Salt Works serves one of the best double cheeseburgers in the area and their homemade onion rings are the perfect side. www.facebook.com/The-Original-Salt-Works-245508413882/
RUNNER UP: Tazy's Burger & Grill features Angus beef burgers served with creative toppings.

BEST RAW BAR: Soundside Seafood & Raw Bar at Wrightsville Beach, www.soundsideseafood.com

BEST STEAK: Port Land Grille has the best steaks in Wilmington hands down, including its 35-day artesian aged Kansas City Strip and Black Angus Cowboy Bone-in Ribeye, www.portlandgrille.com

BEST BBQ: Poor Piggy's BBQ has the best ribs and pulled pork in the area, www.poorpiggys.com

BEST FOOD TRUCK: Catch the Truck from the award-winning chef of Catch restaurant features beef sliders, lobster sliders, and crab cake sliders with cilantro slaw and curry mayo. www.catchthetruck.com

FYI: These listings are only a fraction of the dining and bar options in the greater Wilmington area.

There are hundreds of restaurants, bistros, bars, breweries, coffee shops, diners, and cafes. For a comprehensive and current list of all dining options in the Wilmington area, visit https://www.wilmingtonandbeaches.com/restaurants/all/

BEST GOLF RESORT: Beau Rivage Golf & Resort https://www.beaurivagegolf.com/

BEST GOLF COURSE: Landfall Country Golf, www.countrycluboflandfall.com, **RUNNERS UP: Pine Valley Country Club** and **Cape Fear Country Club**

More Cape Fear Coast Golf Courses: Cape Fear National Golf Course at Brunswick Forest, Bald Head Island Club, Brick Landing Plantation Landing Golf Club, Leopard's Chase Golf Club, and Oak Island Golf Club.

ABOUT ACCOMMODATIONS

Accommodations vary greatly throughout Wilmington and its beach communities. There are many options, such as apartments, beach cottages, resorts, houses, hotels, motels, mansions, and downtown condos.

The best deals will be on vacation rentals or specials found through sites like **www.AirBnB.com, www.vrgo.com www.Priceline.com, www.Trivago.com, https://www.hometogo.com/wilmington-nc/ www.Hotels.com, or www.Booking.com.**

Local Rental Companies

Wilmington Vacation Rentals, www.wilmingtonvacationhomes.com
Wilmington's Best Rentals, www.karenparkin.com
Bryant Real Estate, https://www.bryantre.com/
Intracoastal Vacation Rentals, https://www.intracoastalrentals.com/
Seacoast Rentals, www.seacoastrentals.com

CAMPING

There are several suitable camping options in the Wilmington area. It is advisable to book in advance, especially during big festivals, major holidays, and peak season. If bringing pets, be sure to ask upfront about their pet policy and fees.

BEST CAMPING

Wilmington KOA is a big campground with 100 tent and RV sites that is conveniently located five miles from downtown Wilmington and eight miles from Wrightsville Beach. Open year round with sewer hook-ups, 50 amp power, electric, cable TV and Wi-Fi are available. Amenities include a pool, camping store, computer/TV room, camping store, pet playground, bike rentals, firepit and firewood, laundry room, kid playground and games, pavilion, propane, a "kamping kitchen" and more. https://koa.com/campgrounds/wilmington/

More Campgrounds

Winner's RV Park (Carolina Beach) features 21 spaces with full hook-ups, cable TV, Wi-Fi, and an on-site boat or RV storage lot.

Carolina Beach Family Campground has 100 tent and RV sites with electric, sewer, and water hook-ups, as well as Wi-Fi and cable TV. Amenities include an in-ground pool with sunbathing area, laundry room, large bathhouse and general store. Two riverfront parks are within easy walking distance.

Freeman Park (Carolina Beach) offers primitive camping with tent sites, restrooms, and nearby public beach access.

Carolina Beach State Park is one of the largest and most popular state parks in the Cape Fear area. Their campground features 83 RV and tent sites with sewer, water and 50 amp electric service. Amenities include hiking trails, a boat launch, picnic areas, kayaking, a visitor's center, and an on-site beach.

Woodside RV & Trailer Park (Holly Ridge) features full hook-ups for every site, as well as Wi-Fi, camp store, laundry room, game room, pool, playground, basketball court, and volleyball court.

BEST RESORT: Holiday Inn Resort Wilmington-Wrightsville Beach has three pools (indoor and outside) with poolside service, two whirlpools, a playground, fitness center, two restaurants, bike rentals, lounge, convenience store, and concierge service. Not only do most rooms have balconies overlooking Wrightsville beach, but also have large flat-screen TVs, free Wi-Fi, coffeemakers, microwaves, mini-refrigerators, and in-room safes. Plus, they offer pillow menus, black out shades, and more! https://www.ihg.com/holidayinnresorts/hotels/us/en/wrightsville-beach/

BEST HOSTEL: **Stella Maris Hostel** is a 141-year-old hostel conveniently located in the historic district. It's not fancy but it is comfortable. https://hostelstellamaris.com/

BEST BOUTIQUE HOTEL: Dreamers Welcome is the ultimate in luxury with different themed suites to choose from, including The Dreamer, The Visionary, The Romantic, and The Traveler. My favorite is The Dreamer, which has a private garden entrance that opens

into a big living room complete with kitchenette, dining area, sofa bed, and hanging chair. A separate bedroom features hardwood floors, a custom-designed king-sized bed, and more garden views. The en-suite bathroom includes a clawfoot tub, designer double sink, and rain shower.
https://www.dreamerswelcome.com/downtown
RUNNER UP: Hotel Riverwalk
http://riverwalk.hotels-in-wilmington.com/

BEST FAMILY-FRIENDLY HOTEL: Hampton Inn Wilmington Downtown is perfect for families because it is conveniently located at the riverfront within walking distance of restaurants and museums. It has an indoor pool, complimentary hot breakfast, free Wi-Fi, large flat-screen TVs, and is very reasonably priced despite being a Hilton property in downtown Wilmington (ask about their special discount rates). Rooms have mini-refrigerators and microwaves so you can keep snacks and drinks on hand. Pet-friendly rooms, connecting rooms, and suites are available.

www.hilton.com/e/hotels/ilmdohx-hampton-wilmington-downton/
RUNNER UP: Best Western Coastline Inn is right on the riverfront so it is ideally situated for shopping and sightseeing. The property offers a complimentary full breakfast and pets are welcome for a fee. Rooms are reasonably priced and children 18 and under are free in room with one paying adult. www.bestwestern.com

BEST SUITE HOTEL: Staybridge Suites Wilmington East has a fitness center, guest laundry room, free Wi-Fi, and complimentary breakfast. The suites are large and include fully equipped kitchens.
www.ihg.com/staybridge/hotels/us/en/wilmington/ **RUNNER UP: Springhill Suites by Marriott** is an all-suite property that is conveniently located at the Mayfaire Town Center and offers free buffet breakfast, outdoor pool, convenience store, fitness center, laundry, complimentary tea and coffee, and complimentary parking. www.marriott.com/en-

us/hotels/ilmsh-springhill-suites-wilmington-mayfaire/

BEST BEACH HOTEL: Shell Island Resort at Wrightsville Beach offers all oceanfront/beachfront suites with balconies, plus an outdoor pool, hot tub, and pool bar. Each suite can accommodate up to six people with one bedroom (one king or two doubles), 1.5 baths, and living room with sleeper sofa, dining area, and kitchenette. Large flat screen TVs are in the bedroom and living room. There is also a restaurant and lounge in the resort, plus a tiki bar during the summer. Be sure to check special deals and packages offered exclusively online. www.shellisland.com

RUNNER UP: Courtyard by Marriott Carolina Beach has heated indoor and outdoor pools, fitness center, laundry room, free Wi-Fi, and completely renovated rooms and suites that are all oceanfront. There is a Starbucks® and a bistro on the property, but it is also within walking distance to many dining options.

www.marriott.com/en-us/hotels/ilmcb-courtyard-carolina-beach

BEST EXTENDED STAY HOTEL:
Staybridge Suites Wilmington East has a fitness center, guest laundry room, free Wi-Fi, and complimentary breakfast. The large suites include fully equipped kitchens.
www.ihg.com/staybridge/hotels/us/en/wilmington/

Best Pet-Friendly: Residence Inn by Marriott Wilmington Landfall feature large apartment-style suites, adjacent to the prestigious Landfall community. There are many dining, shopping, and entertainment options nearby. Amenities include a lovely verandah with rocking chairs, free full hot breakfast, free tea and coffee, free parking, convenience store, fitness center, laundry room, gas grills if you'd like to cookout, landscaped courtyard, gatehouse, pool, Sport Court, pond, and putting green. The studios and suites are large yet cozy. Pets are welcome for a fee. www.marriott.com/en-us/hotels/ilmri-residence-inn-wilmington-landfall/

RUNNERS UP: Staybridge Suites Wilmington, Days Inn by Wydham Wilmington, Best Western Coastline, and **Best Western Wilmington.**

FYI: Be sure to call the hotel to add your pet(s) if you book online.

BEST RIVERWALK HOTEL: Aloft Wilmington at Coastline Center offers free tea and coffee, convenience store, laundry room, great outdoor space with firepit, fitness center, restaurant, rainfall showers, and ultra-plush bedding & linen. www.marriott.com/en-us/hotels/ilmal-aloft-wilmington-at-coastline-center/

BEST ROMANTIC HOTEL: Dreamers Welcome offers oversized bay windows overlooking the garden, huge en-suite bathroom with a rain shower and a claw foot tub, hand-carved fireplace, high vaulted ceilings, glass bar cart that can be wheeled anywhere in the room, and a velvet queen-size bed.
www.dreamerswelcome.com

BEST HISTORIC HOTEL/INN: Graystone Inn was originally "The Bridgers Mansion," (built 1905-1906). It is a historic landmark and one of the most distinguished structures in Wilmington. Graystone Inn has maintained its charm despite extensive renovations to ensure complete guest satisfaction. Guests will sleep well on the luxurious linens and bedding. Fine dining is available on site, as well as a cozy reading room with fireplace.
https://stayatthegraystone.com/

BEST AMBIENCE: C.W. Worth House Bed & Breakfast is a quaint B&B housed inside a historic Victorian mansion that is filled with period antiques and cozy fireplaces. The themed guest rooms have a sitting area, slumber sound machine, private bath, plush bathrobes, and luxury bedding. You may want to enjoy a sundowner in their garden after a long day of sightseeing. Each day starts off with a full English, Irish, or American breakfast with specialty tea and coffee included. Free Wi-Fi and parking is included, as well as complimentary refreshment stations on each floor. The inn is located in the historic district so it is easy walking distance to the Downtown Riverfront. www.worthhouse.com

The Hive

BEST APARTMENT HOTEL: The Hive is one of the coolest hotels in Wilmington with its eclectic, hipster style. There is funky artwork, exposed brick, mismatching furniture, woven textiles, and lots of color throughout. Guest rooms have comfy couches, 55" 4K TVs, free Wi-Fi, large showers, and full-size kitchens. It is in the heart of downtown Wilmington, www.thehivewilmington.com

BEST BUDGET HOTEL: Baymont Inn & Suites is a budget hotel that doesn't feel like one because it is a Wyndham property. It has a free hot or cold breakfast daily in its large Breakfast Corner Station, free parking, free newspapers, free Wi-Fi, free coffee, pool, fitness center, and is close to area attractions. Rooms and suites are available and if you are a member of their loyalty rewards program you can earn free stays. www.wyndhamhotels.com/baymont/wilmington-north-carolina/

RUNNERS UP: Best Western Plus Wilmington Wrightsville Beach and **Hampton Inn & Suites Wrightsville Beach**

BEST Adults Only: Woodspring Suites Wilmington has affordable nightly, weekly, or monthly rates. They offer different suite sizes and styles (all with kitchens and dining table with chairs) and are also pet friendly. There is free parking, large laundry room, free Wi-Fi, and flat screen TVs with cable/satellite. www.woodspring.com

Best B&B: The Verandas has a garden terrace, two parlors, and multiple verandas. The guest rooms are so inviting you won't want to leave! Complimentary wine and cookies are served in the afternoon. A gourmet breakfast with specialty coffee or tea is served daily in their formal dining room. It is located in the historic district so it is very convenient to shopping, sites, and dining. www.verandas.com

RUNNER UP: Port City Guest House is also in the historic district and has free parking, a garden, free Wi-Fi, complimentary refreshments every afternoon, and a full American breakfast is served in their dining room. Discounts offered to teachers, seniors, and veterans. www.portcityguesthouse.com

Best Inn: Taylor House Inn serves a daily candlelight breakfast with crystal and fine china in the formal dining room. The foyer, parlor, and front porch with rockers and swings are cozy and inviting. Check their website for current specials and to choose your themed room. www.taylorhousebb.com

ABOUT WILMINGTON

Wilmington was first inhabited by various Native American tribes until it was discovered in the late 16th century by explorer, Giovanni da Verrazano.

The area was colonized in the 1720s when an English settlement was established. By the 1730s, the area along the riverfront was named "New Town," but by 1740 the name had changed to Wilmington in honor of Spencer

Compton, the Earl of Wilmington in England.

Wilmington grew and prospered, thanks to its proximity to the Cape Fear River. Soon this small settlement was a bustling port community.

Wilmington was the first armed resistance against the British, with their protest of the Stamp Act of 1765. They abducted the stamp master and forced him to resign. Wilmington played a critical role during the Revolutionary War because it had become a major port. Wilmington was the largest city and the biggest port in North Carolina at the time of the American Revolution.

On Sunday, January 28, 1776, Wilmington discovered that two British warships were on their way to Wilmington after trying to retake Fort Johnston (Southport). The town prepared for war, women and children were sent out of town, and martial law was enacted. Anyone who refused to take an oath to support the Patriots was forced to work on the fortifications. Twenty professed Loyalists were taken into custody.

Royal Governor Josiah Martin (the last British governor of North Carolina), who had been forced to flee New Bern the previous summer, was aboard one of the two warships, the *HMS Cruzier*. He was trying to slip past Wilmington to get to Cross Creek, where a Loyalist army of volunteers had formed. But the Patriots were waiting with cannons and guns. The ships tried to go around Eagle Island but the water was too shallow. The British were forced to retreat. However, there were other minor skirmishes and events that took place in this area during the American Revolution, such as the

Battle of Moores Creek Bridge and a battle at Brunswick Town in 1776. In 1781, Wilmington was occupied by British troops under the command of Lord Cornwallis.

Like everywhere else, the war took a toll on Wilmington. But after it was over, Wilmington grew and prospered in the late 1700s and well into the 1800s. A railroad connecting Wilmington to the state capital, Raleigh, was a big part of that growth. When the railroad was completed in 1840, it was longest single railroad track in the world at the time.

A major yellow fever epidemic claimed the lives of 654 Wilmington residents in 1862.

During the Civil War, Wilmington was strategically important once again because of its proximity to the Cape Fear River and its status as a major port. Prior to the war, rice, peanuts, cotton, and naval stores left this port for destinations all over the world. During the war, the profitable enterprise of blockade-running sprang up in Wilmington. The only way the Confederacy survived for so long was the military armaments and supplies that came into this port. English and Scottish merchants transported luxury items and war goods back and forth to the West Indies via steamer ships.

For the majority of the Civil War, Wilmington was held by the Confederacy, but fell to Union troops after the second Battle of Fort Fisher. The attack on Fort Fisher was the largest amphibious attack by US forces until Normandy during World War II.

The First Battle of Fort Fisher was a naval siege when the Union first tried to capture the fort. It lasted from December 23–27, 1864. The

Union navy tried to detonate a ship filled with gun powder in order to demolish the fort's walls but this failed. Next, the navy launched a two-day bombardment on the fort. On the second day, the Union army started landing troops for their attack. But before he could implement his plan, Major General Benjamin Butler got word the Confederacy had reinforcements arriving and deteriorating weather conditions. With that news, he made the decision to call off the attack. He was relieved of command on January 8, 1865, and was replaced by Major General Alfred H. Terry, who captured the fort one week later during the second Battle of Fort Fisher.

By this time, Fort Fisher was the last coastal stronghold of the Confederacy. The fort protected blockade running vessels using the Wilmington port. Union troops attacked the fort on January 13th for the second Battle of Fort Fisher, and two days later, the Confederacy surrendered and Fort Fisher came under Union control for the rest of the war.

Nearly 3,000 Confederate and Union troops were lost during the second Battle of Fort Fisher.

The fall of Wilmington ultimately meant the fall of the Confederacy and the war ended just months after Wilmington was captured by Union troops.

The Wilmington Insurrection of 1898

(also known as the Wilmington Race Riots of 1898) was a major racial conflict and remains one of the darkest chapters in the town's history.

When the 20th century was ushered in, it brought with it WWI and WWII. Three prisoner-of-war (POW) camps operated in the city during WWII from February 1944 through April 1946. The camps held as many as many as 550 German prisoners.

The North Carolina Shipbuilding Company was a major industry for Wilmington during the 1940s.They employed thousands of workers and built 243 war ships.

The State Port Authority was approved in 1945. In 1947, the University of North Carolina Wilmington was established. The first N.C. Azalea Festival was held the following year. The Cape Fear Community College (formerly the

Wilmington Industrial Education Center) opened in 1958. In 1961, the *USS Battleship NC,* the only American battleship to take part in all 12 major naval offensives in the Pacific during World War II, arrived in Wilmington. It is permanently moored on the Wilmington waterfront. It is one of the most visited tourist attractions in the Wilmington area.

By the late 20th century, Wilmington's biggest industry was tourism. Interstate 40 opened in 1990, linking Raleigh and the rest of North Carolina to Wilmington. Also during the late 20th century, Wilmington became known as "Wilmywood" and "Hollywood of the East," thanks to Screen Gem Studios. It opened in Wilmington and to this day remains the largest movie studio in America outside of Hollywood. More than 400 movies and television shows have been filmed here.

Wilmington is known for many things, such as its antebellum architecture, historic district, its impressive seaport, the University of North Carolina Wilmington, Cape Fear Community College, and Gem Studios.

It's also a major financial center with more than sixty state, regional, and national banks in Wilmington. Health care and manufacturing are also major industries. Tourism also has a huge economic impact. Out of 100 North Carolina counties, New Hanover County ranks #8 for highest amount spent by tourists. It is one of the top ten tourist destinations in North Carolina. Wilmington tourism accounted for $659 million in revenue in 2019. The travel & tourism industry employs nearly 7,000 people. The Wilmington

Convention Center, located on the riverfront, is the largest, boutique convention center on the North Carolina coast.

FYI: The Greater Wilmington Chamber of Commerce is the oldest Chamber in North Carolina, dating back to 1853.

The Wilmington Convention Center is 107,000 square feet.

However, its biggest industry may be the seaport. Recently, the Port of Wilmington welcomed its largest container ship to date, setting a new record. The ship, the *Yang Ming*

Warranty, was carrying 14,220 TEUs (twenty-foot equivalent units). This was the second time in recent history that the 284-acre port set a record for the largest ship to stop in Wilmington. In addition to being an international seaport, the Port of Wilmington is home to several industries making medical, electrical, clothing, paper products, pharmaceuticals, and telecommunications equipment. The Port of Wilmington brings in nearly $13 billion for the state. And this figure doesn't even include the thousands of jobs or taxes earned from the port!

The Port of Wilmington is a 284-acre full service, deep water port, making it the biggest in the state.

ANNUAL EVENTS & AVERAGE TEMPS

Wilmington is a year-round town, meaning there is always something going on, especially during the spring, summer, and weekends. Here is a list of some of the biggest and best. Some are free and some cost to participate. A comprehensive list and more details can be found at https://www.capefearnc.com/events.html

January

New Year celebrations (various locations)

February

NC Jazz Festival

March

Wrightsville Beach Marathon & Half Marathon

Azalea Sprint (Wilmington)

Poplar Grove Herb & Garden Fair (Poplar Grove Plantation)

Annual CFCC Riverfront Boat Show (Wilmington)

April

NC Azalea Festival dates back to 1948 and is one of the biggest events of the year. This five-day event will bring nearly 250,000 visitors to Wilmington to celebrate the Queen Azalea coronation, a shag dance contest, parade, fun run, street fair, arts show, fireworks, nightly concerts, and more.

NC Azalea Festival Historic Home Tour

Cape Fear Garden Club Azalea Garden Tour

Carolina Cup (Wrightsville Beach)

Kure Beach Street Festival

NC Science Festival

Wilmington's Jewish Film Festival

May

Carolina Beach Street Arts Festival Hang

Annual Orange Street ArtsFest

Wilmington Exchange Festival

Memorial Day Weekend Celebration

Battleship NC Memorial Day Observance

June

Carolina Beach Music Festival

Anniversary of the Battle of Fort Fisher

Flag Day at *Battleship NC*

Wilmington Summer Concert Series

July

NC Fourth of July Festival (Southport) is the biggest celebration on the Cape Fear Coast

Wilmington Summer Concert Series

Feast Down East 4th of July

August

Wilmington Summer Concert Series

September

Carolina Beach Inshore Challenge (fishing competition)

Dragon Boat Regatta & Festival (Carolina Beach)

Pier-to-Pier Swim (Wrightsville Beach)

October

Riverfest is a free event that has been around since 1979. Thousands of tourists flock to Wilmington to enjoy this fun event.

Bark in the Park

Voracious Rare Beer Festival

Pleasure Island Surf Fishing Challenge (Carolina Beach)

Oktoberfest (various locations)

Iron Man 70.3 (big deal triathlon event)

Lighthouse Beer & Wine Festival

Pleasure Island Seafood, Blues, & Jazz Festival

November

Cape Fear Kite Festival (Kure Beach)

Cape Fear Festival of Trees (Fort Fisher)

Battleship NC Marathon (Half, 5K, 10K)

Cucalorus Film Festival (one of the largest and most renowned film festivals in America)

Enchanted Airlie (a holiday highlight)

NC Holiday Flotilla at Wrightsville Beach

Taste of Wrightsville Beach

Kure Beach Holiday Market

December

Enchanted Airlie

Cape Fear Festival of Trees (NC Aquarium at Fort Fisher)

FYI: Hurricane Season is June 1 – November 30. An average of 2.3 major tropical storms affect North Carolina each year with one every other year making a direct hit. Hurricane Florence (2018) was one of the worst storms to hit the area.

Also, this is the beach, so bugs (especially mosquitos) are prevalent in the summer months.

It is sunny 216 days of the year (The U.S. average is 202). It gets 58" of rainfall on average annually (The U.S. average is 38"). The driest month is April (2.94") and the wettest month is July (8"). Not surprisingly, the coldest month is January and the hottest month is July.

Average Temps

The best time to visit Wilmington is in the spring (March to May) and in the fall (September to November) when temperatures are mild and hurricanes are less likely, especially in the spring. But early summer and late summer are good times, as well. Below is a list of average temperatures but realistically you will experience closer to 90° here in July.

Peak time to visit is the summer months, but be forewarned that it is HOT and HUMID late June to late August (and most crowded).

Month	**High / Low (°F)**	
AVERAGE TEMPS		
January	56° / 38°	46°
February	59° / 40°	48°
March	66° / 46°	55°
April	73° / 54°	63°
May	80° / 60°	70°
June	86° / 70°	77°
July	88° / 75°	80°
August	87° / 72°	79°
September	82° / 67°	74°
October	75° / 56°	65°
November	67° / 47°	56°
December	60° / 42°	49°

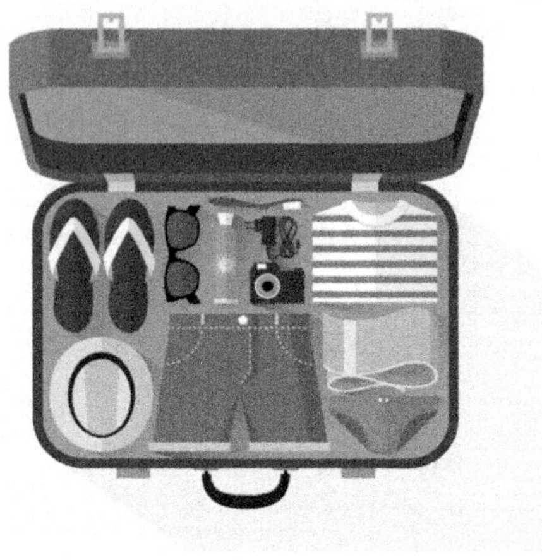

How to Pack

Like most coastal communities, the Wilmington area is casual dress for the most part so it is easy to pack:

*shorts

*sandals/flip flops/beach shoes

*walking shoes

*gear (fishing rod, scuba mask, surfboard, floats, pool noodles, boogie boards, etc.)

*bathing suit(s) and cover up

*t-shirts

*lightweight pants

*resort casual 'dress' clothes (if plan to dine at upscale restaurant or enjoy the nightlife)

*30 SPF sunscreen and hat

*insect repellent

*rain jacket or windbreaker

*light sweater (if you are cold-natured you may want one in places where the A/C is working well)

*waterproof bag (to safeguard phone, camera, wallet, etc.)

*toiletries and cosmetics (be sure to pack these items in a zippered bag or at least put liquid items in a Ziploc bag so that there are no spills or leaks on your clothes or electronics)

*medications (make sure you have enough for three days longer than your trip, just in case you are delayed for any reason)

*documents

*extra batteries, sim cards, flash drives, cords and/or chargers

*entertainment (device loaded with games, eBooks, and shows/movies or bring books, playing cards, DVDs, and old-fashioned board games.

FYI: Take pictures on your phone of all tickets and confirmations, just in case you lose the originals.

TERRANCE ZEPKE
Series Reading Order & Guide

Series List

Most Haunted Series

Terrance Talks Travel Series

Cheap Travel Series

Spookiest Series

Strange Series

Weird & Wonderful Travels

Stop Talking Series

Carolinas for Kids Series Ghosts of the Carolinas Series

Books & Guides for the Carolinas Series

& More Books by Terrance Zepke

Introduction

Here is a list of titles by Terrance Zepke. They are presented in chronological order although they do not need to be read in any particular order.

Also included is an author bio, a personal message from Terrance, and some other information you may find helpful.

Most books are available in digital and print formats. They can be found on all major booksellers or ordered through your favorite independent bookseller.

For more about this author and her books visit her Author Page at: http://www.amazon.com/Terrance-Zepke/e/B000APJNIA/.

You can also connect with Terrance on Twitter @terrancezepke or on

www.facebook.com/terrancezepke
www.pinterest.com/terrancezepke
www.goodreads.com/terrancezepke

Sign up for weekly email notifications of the ***Terrance Talks Travel*** blog and receive a FREE 50-page CHEAP TRAVEL REPORT and be the first to learn about new episodes of Uber Adventures, cheap travel tips & resources, and her TRIP PICK OF THE WEEK at www.terrancetalkstravel.com or sign up for her ***Mostly Ghostly*** blog at www.terrancezepke.com.

≈

TERRANCE TALKS TRAVEL

You can follow her travel show, **TERRANCE TALKS TRAVEL: ÜBER ADVENTURES on** www.blogtalkradio.com/terrancetalkstravel or subscribe to it on **iTunes.**

Warning: Listening to this show could lead to a spectacular South African safari, hot-air ballooning over the Swiss Alps, Disney Adventures, and Tornado Tours!

≈

AUTHOR BIO

Terrance Zepke studied Journalism at the University of Tennessee and later received a Master's degree in Mass Communications from the University of South Carolina. And she studied parapsychology at the renowned Rhine Research Center.

Zepke spends much of her time happily traveling around the world but always returns home to the Carolinas where she lives part-time in both states. She has written hundreds of articles and more than fifty books. She is also the host of *Terrance Talks Travel: Über Adventures.* Additionally, this award-winning and best-selling author has been featured in many publications and programs, such as NPR, CNN, *The Washington Post*, *Adventure Journal*, Associated Press, Travel with Rick Steves, Around the World, *Publishers Weekly*, *Woman's Day*, World Travel & Dining with Pierre Wolfe, Good Morning Show, The Learning Channel, and The Travel Channel.

When she's not investigating haunted places, searching for pirate treasure, or climbing lighthouses, she is most likely packing for her next adventure to some far flung place, such as Reykjavik or Kwazulu Natal. Some of her favorite adventures include piranha fishing on the Amazon, shark cage diving in South Africa, hiking the Andes Mountains Inca Trail, camping in the Himalayas, dog-sledding in the Arctic Circle, and a gorilla safari in the Congo.

MOST HAUNTED SERIES

A Ghost Hunter's Guide to the Most Haunted Places in America

A Ghost Hunter's Guide to the Most Haunted Houses in America

A Ghost Hunter's Guide to the Most Haunted Hotels & Inns in America

A Ghost Hunter's Guide to the Most Haunted Historic Sites in America

A Ghost Hunter's Guide to the Most Haunted Places in the World

The Ghost Hunter's MOST HAUNTED Box Set (3 in 1): Discover America's Most Haunted Destinations

MOST HAUNTED and SPOOKIEST Sampler Box Set: Featuring *A GHOST HUNTER'S GUIDE TO THE MOST HAUNTED PLACES IN AMERICA* and *SPOOKIEST CEMETERIES*

TERRANCE TALKS TRAVEL SERIES

Terrance Talks Travel: A Pocket Guide to South Africa

Terrance Talks Travel: A Pocket Guide to African Safaris

Terrance Talks Travel: A Pocket Guide to Adventure Travel

Terrance Talks Travel: A Pocket Guide to Florida Keys (including Key West & The Everglades)

Terrance Talks Travel: The Quirky Tourist Guide to Key West

Terrance Talks Travel: The Quirky Tourist Guide to Cape Town

Terrance Talks Travel: The Quirky Tourist Guide to Reykjavik (Iceland)

Terrance Talks Travel: The Quirky Tourist Guide to Charleston, South Carolina

Terrance Talks Travel: The Quirky Tourist Guide to Ushuaia (The Gateway to Antarctica)

Terrance Talks Travel: The Quirky Tourist Guide to Antarctica

Terrance Talks Travel: The Quirky Tourist Guide to Machu Picchu & Cuzco (Peru)

Terrance Talks Travel: A Pocket Guide to East Africa's Uganda and Rwanda

Terrance Talks Travel: The Quirky Tourist Guide to Kathmandu (Nepal) & The Himalayas

Terrance Talks Travel: The Quirky Tourist Guide to Edinburgh, Scotland

Terrance Talks Travel: The Quirky Tourist Guide to Marrakesh, Morocco

Terrance Talks Travel: The Quirky Tourist Guide to Myrtle Beach, South Carolina

Terrance Talks Travel: The Quirky Tourist Guide to Savannah, Georgia

Terrance Talks Travel: A Pocket Guide to New Zealand

Terrance Talks Travel: The Quirky Tourist Guide to Queensland, Australia

Terrance Talks Travel: The Quirky Tourist Guide to Sydney, Australia

Terrance Talks Travel: The Quirky Tourist Guide to Lapland (Arctic Circle) & Helsinki, Finland

Terrance Talks Travel: Cheap London

Terrance Talks Travel: Cheap Disney

Terrance Talks Travel: The Quirky Tourist Guide to Amsterdam

Terrance Talks Travel: Cheap Las Vegas

Terrance Talks Travel: The Quirky Tourist Guide to the Outer Banks, North Carolina

Terrance Talks Travel: The Quirky Tourist Guide to Wilmington & the Cape Fear Coast, North Carolina

African Safari Box Set: Featuring TERRANCE TALKS TRAVEL: *A Pocket Guide to South Africa* and *TERRANCE TALKS TRAVEL: A Pocket Guide to African Safaris*

CHEAP TRAVEL SERIES

How to Cruise Cheap!

How to Fly Cheap!

How to Travel Cheap!

How to Travel FREE or Get Paid to Travel!

CHEAP TRAVEL SERIES (4 IN 1) BOX SET (2017)

≈

SPOOKIEST SERIES

Spookiest Lighthouses

Spookiest Battlefields

Spookiest Cemeteries

Spookiest Objects

Spookiest Military Bases, Ships, Museums, & Forts

Spookiest Box Set (3 in 1): Discover America's Most Haunted Destinations (Spookiest Lighthouses, Spookiest Battlefields & Spookiest Cemeteries)

MOST HAUNTED and SPOOKIEST Sampler Box Set: Featuring *A GHOST HUNTER'S GUIDE TO THE MOST HAUNTED PLACES IN AMERICA* and *SPOOKIEST CEMETERIES*

≈

WEIRD & WONDERFUL TRAVEL SERIES

The World's Weirdest Museums

The World's Weirdest Attractions

The World's Weirdest Accommodations

≈

STRANGE SERIES

The Most Cursed Places in the World

The Creepiest Places in the World
(Coming Soon!)

≈

STOP TALKING SERIES

Stop Talking & Start Writing Your Book

Stop Talking & Start Publishing Your Book

Stop Talking & Start Selling Your Book

Stop Talking & Start Writing Your Book Series (3 in 1) Box Set (Writing, Publishing & Selling Your Book)

BOOKS ABOUT THE CAROLINAS

Lighthouses of the Carolinas for Kids
Pirates of the Carolinas for Kids
Ghosts of the Carolinas for Kids
Ghosts of the Carolina Coasts
The Best Ghost Tales of South Carolina
Ghosts & Legends of the Carolina Coasts
The Best Ghost Tales of North Carolina
Pirates of the Carolinas
Lighthouses of the Carolinas: A Short History & Guide

MORE BOOKS

Lowcountry Voodoo: Tales, Spells & Boo Hags

Happy Halloween! Hundreds of Perfect Party Recipes, Delightful Decorating Ideas & Awesome Activities

Ghosts of Savannah

How to Train Your Puppy or Dog Using Three Simple Strategies (FUN & FAST!)

*Fiction books are written under a pseudonym.

Message from the Author

The primary purpose of this guide is to introduce you to some titles you may not have known about. Another reason for it is to let you know all the ways you can connect with me. Authors love to hear from readers. We truly appreciate you more than you'll ever know. Please feel free to send me a comment or question via the comment form found on every page on www.terrancezepke.com and www.terrancetalkstravel.com or follow me on your favorite social media. Don't forget that you can also listen to my travel show, **Terrance Talks Travel: Über Adventures** on Blog Talk Radio, Amazon Podcasts, and iTunes. The best way to make sure you don't miss any episodes of these shows (and find a complete archive of shows), new book releases and giveaways, cheap travel tips, free downloadable travel reports, and more is to subscribe to ***Terrance Talks Travel*** on www.terrancetalkstravel.com or ***Mostly Ghostly*** on www.terrancezepke.com. If you'd like to learn more about any of my books, you can find in-depth descriptions and "look inside" options through most online booksellers.

Thank you for your interest and HAPPY READING!

Terrance

INDEX

C

D

E

F

G

H

O

P

R

S

T

U

W

Y

Z

Made in the USA
Las Vegas, NV
26 June 2022

50746007R10115